Bittersweet Bourbon

Mansi Chauhan

Thank you Sachin for the lovely illustrations and for your sincere proofreading and formatting. Thank you my friend for helping me create this book from scratch, for always being the support I need.

I DEDICATE THIS BOOK TO ALL THE YOUNG
SOULS WHO STRUGGLE TO SPEAK THEIR
MINDS. I HOPE THAT IN THIS BOOK THEY FIND
SOME COMFORT.

Ðear Reader,

Perception is like taste. If you ask about the taste of whiskey from a group of people who are having it, you will almost never get the same answer from everyone. Everyone is drinking from the same bottle, describing according to their best judgment yet everyone's description is different, and perhaps correct. Perception, like taste, is subjective. This is one thing, and before you begin with this book, the other thing which I want to address, is a complex feeling.

The feeling of experiencing all kinds of emotions all together, the intense confusion of the mixed weird emotions when they all start to fuse into one another and then dissolve into a single dark indifferent feeling - numbness. This is the bittersweet feeling which I experience when I sit down to write something as I often find myself struggling to choose the feeling about which I want to write. It has taken me so long to take the shot at writing poetry as for the majority of my early 20s, I have struggled to get past this feeling of "numbness".

I used to draw a lot during my childhood. My drawings were mostly black and white; coloring never fascinated me. In fact, I used to always mess-up my drawings whenever I would decide to make them colorful. I've always had a fear of being discovered and because of this very reason, for a very long time, I also never let anyone discover that I loved singing (except for a few friends).

I have always loved to draw and sing, and with time I have become better at singing but worse at drawing. All those years I have really struggled to speak my mind, and I guess I have somehow wanted to express myself, although not too much.

Long story short, poetry is relatively new to me and every now and then I have made myself to sit and write, hoping to get better with time. I have not categorized or organized my poems because I think the random order of these poems will best depict the unpredictable nature of life, maintaining the overall "bittersweet" theme of this book but like taste, as I explained earlier, it will be subjective. So, how bitter or how sweet you find this book will depend on the type of experiences that you've had. I, on the other hand have tried my best to balance the overall flavor of this concoction which I've further labelled as "Bourbon", as I desire to make it tasteful for each and every one of you. It's unusual for me, but here I am, sharing with you some of my deepest feelings.

I wish you good reading!

Cheers!

CONTENTS

Day and Night

The landscape caught fire.
It was blood orange
With the sun and its blaze.
It began to smell like hot summer days,
And burned ferociously
To slowly progress
To darker shades.
The smoke had risen
To blur the edges
Then thickened with grace
To conceal everything
In its embrace.
It seemed like the work
Of a magic spell,
As everything had charred,
But stars in the night sky
Dimly glowed,
Some said, "They are fighting hard".

Their brightness
Was not enough,
So as to clearly trace
The journey's end,
But the travelers did still
Reach where they had to,
Finding directions
In their constellations.

WILDERNESS

Aqua, olive, mustard, mulberry
And other iridescent colors in play,
Are together painting a scenery,
Bewitched by the wilderness
As I survey,
Embracing the solitude,
There I lay.
The blooming wildflowers
Catch my eye
As I stop by the riverside,
Sunlight filtering through the trees nearby,
Where grasslands stretch
Beneath the sky,
And oh! I love the butterflies.

DAYDREAMING

It has been a while since I enjoyed
My favorite sweet with cardamom chai.
It has been a while since I did it while
Listening to the favorite songs of mine.
I miss the raindrops touching my skin
As they fall close to my feet,
When I sit under my front porch.
I miss the time in my garden,
Where I riffled through the pages
Of my favorite books.
I'll have to catch up
As I'm missing out on a lot of feelings.
All I do is think about them,
All I end up with is daydreaming.

APPREHENSION

My favorite street.
It's wide; gives me space.
It's quiet; I can listen to
My heartbeats and footsteps.
It's long; I can stroll forever.
Oh! so many people.
Faces, I've never seen.
Voices, unknown to me.
I wanted to find a refuge,
But I think it was better inside.
Apprehension has crushed my gut
Yet again.

Corruption

Must have been a lie.
How beautiful the world seemed,
Through the eyes
Of a curious child!
It got uglier each day
And now it looks as dull as grey,
Only to soon rot away.

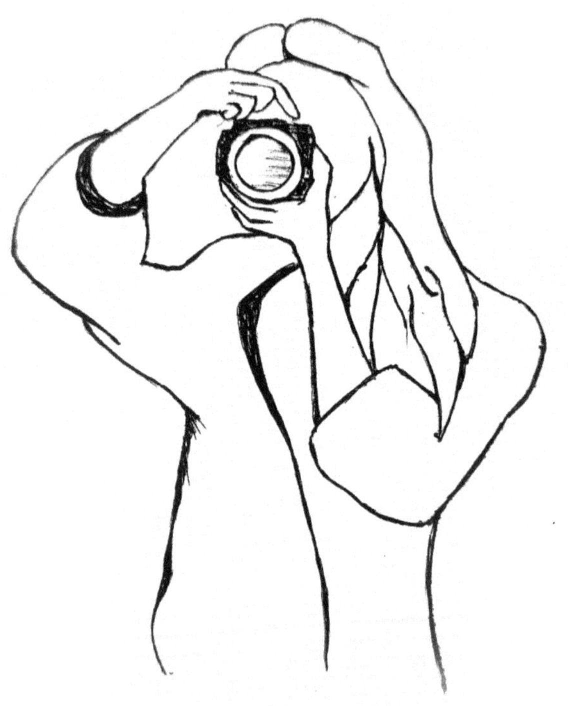

A PUZZLED PHOTOGRAPHER

Drawing smiling faces
On the foggy windows
Makes them forget
All the times they cried,
Sleeping on the footpath
On their backs they lie,
Thinking to themselves,
They have all the sky.
With no shoes to wear
They run like the wind,
Barefoot but boisterous,
And they joyfully sing.
Selling newspapers everyday
They keep afloat,
And with the dirty old ones
They make paper-boats.
Do they still crave
Expensive toys,
When all the magic
Is in their minds?

Ðo they really need
A helping hand,
When on their own
They're more than fine?
Puzzled by these children
Of misfortune,
Who make castles with the rubble
They find on the streets,
Wonders the photographer,
"What do I know!",
Trying to capture the emotions
So bittersweet.

DEATH OF A POET

A life's story
Is getting washed away
With each drop of tear running down
Into the puddle of her sorrows,
Making daunting ripples
Dance around.
And, colors of the painting
Which once described her face,
Are beginning to sink
In this melting disgrace.
She plunges her feet
From where they bled,
To wash her wounds
In the puddle of tears.
The waters have now
Turned blood red
And her red reflection
Is locked in fear.

She's shocked to see
How the red of her wounds
Has vanquished the entire color palette
Of her existence.
She can't help but think, "What a waste!,
When I could have used it as ink
To write down
My reminiscence".

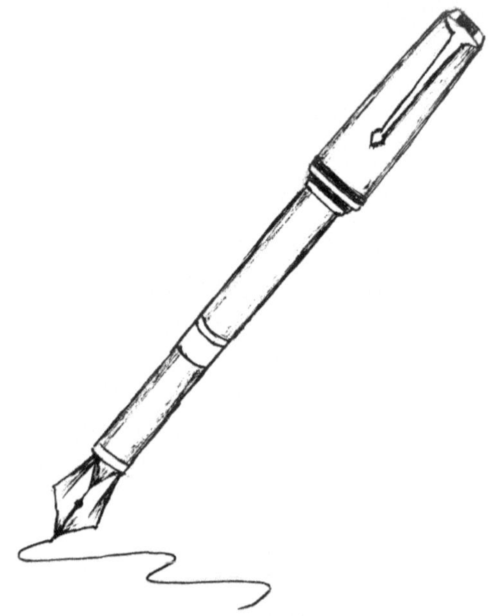

STATE OF MY HEART

This wind which comes

Occasionally,

Has brought with it,

Melancholy,

And, what was set to transform

Into a perfect storm,

Just ignited the sparks

Of my beloved artform.

A memory of someone

Once drifted apart,

Was invigorated passionately

and turned into art.

I shall write with sincerity,

Each and every part.

I shall bring to life

The state of my heart.

DELUSION

What is it to love you?
What must I call it?
Peace or commotion,
Or solely satisfaction?
Is it to quench my yearning for
The freedom from desolation or
Is it hypnotism?
Because it feels as if there's nothing
In this never ending nothingness,
But you.
What is this delusion?
Knowingly being inside
The unseen and unfelt,
Holding the hand of my conscience,
Following a weird melody,
And moving forward
Into the subsequent uncertainty.
How come I'm living a reality
Which gradually fades into a dream,
Again and again?
My lover, emancipate me from this pain.

PART OF ME

I took you everyday,
A little in each breath.
Now you flow in my veins
As part of me.

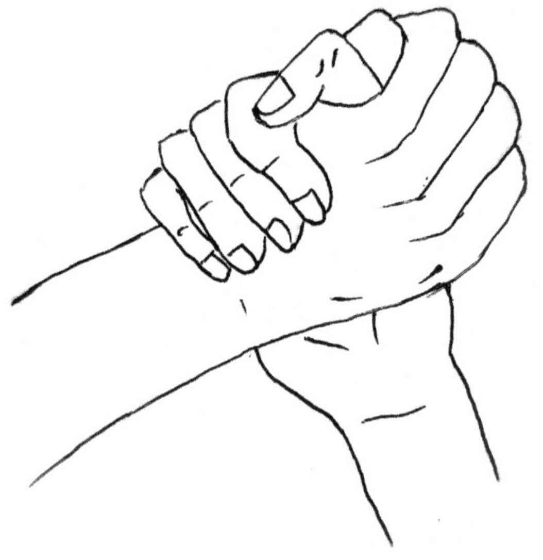

CHOICE

How did you decide
To put everyone aside
And hold my hand
To pull me from outside
Of this pool of fire
Which had kept from imploding,
My shrinking pride,
But burning me inch by inch,
Until I would cede and chide?
How did you, unlike everyone
Saw me differently,
And refused to abide
The cacophonic voice
That pompously prophesied,
I would be no one's
First choice?

Uncomfortable

The moment I start talking
About something passionately,
I see people getting uncomfortable.
It's like they are saying;
Good to know, but not too much,
Good to say, but not too much,
But why should I dumb down?
Why do they resent my eloquence?
Is it only my responsibility
To always be polite and humble?
Or their interrupting me mid sentence,
Is nothing but a week attempt
To save their fragile ego?

Inheritance

I experienced separation
Much before I could discover relationships.
I endured grief
Much before I could discover joy.
I learned to wipe away my tears
Much before I could laugh my heart out.
It took me long to habituate to happiness,
For I inherited only pain.

SHAREHOLDERS

The burden of a family name.
Even my mistakes aren't mine alone to claim.
They warn, they'll also have to face the blame.
Blood relations declare and announce
What's right and what's wrong.
So that I could conveniently be tamed.
If I do right then it's all good.
If I go wrong then I am shamed.
Oh! The burden of a family name.

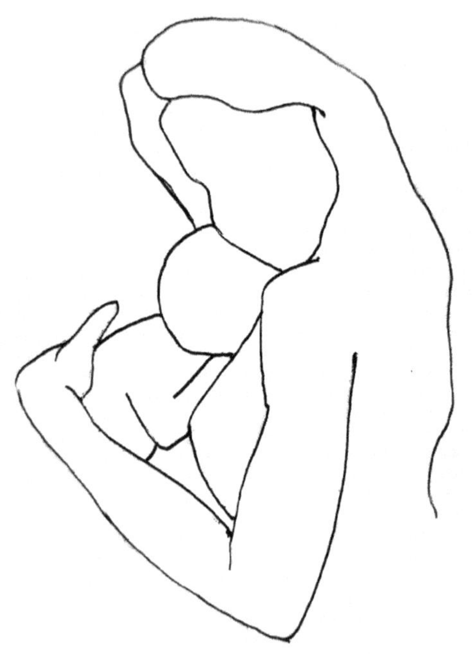

MOTHER

Her insightful eyes
Which didn't let her rest,
Struggled, suffered and settled
For crow's feet.
Her pretentious smile
Which didn't let me know
The pain it steadily mastered
To defeat.
As right as rain,
She has been there,
In all my battles,
Fighting more than me.
I owe so much,
But can never repay
What my mother
Has done for me.

MEMORIES

Life is a long list of moments,
That you keep safe as memories.
Happy, sad or bittersweet,
They play in your head like songs
from a saved playlist on repeat.

Bad Memories

A bad memory, like an old wound
Starts to itch
As it gets brushed
And you keep scratching it,
Until it bleeds
Again.
A bad memory, like criticism
Stays with you,
And in all bad situations
It makes sure
To make you remember itself
Again.
A bad memory, like the stink
Of a rotten dead animal,

Lingers around,
And all bad smells remind you of it
And it becomes afresh
Again.
A bad memory, like loneliness,
Seeks you in disguise
Of comfort, peace, inception or maturity,
But never leaves
And you find yourself miserable
Again.

Good Memories

A good memory is like the flavor
Of your favorite ice cream.
It's something
That you know
You will crave for,
Again.
A good memory, like walking barefoot
On dewy grass, is something
You can't resist once you see it.
You'd want to enjoy
The way it makes you feel
Again.
A good memory is like that special moment
When you see your friend
Waving at you from a distance.

Moments like these

Bring you joy again and

Again.

A good memory, like an inside joke,

Will find it's way randomly

Into your conversations,

And whenever you're alone

It will bring a smile on your face

Again.

A LONELY LITTLE HOUSE

If I could travel back in time,
I would go back to the lonely little house
Surrounded by green valleys,
Where I once used to belong.
The house was painted white
With subtle red details.
The house was full of grace
Coz' once it accepted a little girl,
Born at an awkward timing, unfortunately.
As opposed to bringing joy,
She had brought a pile of responsibilities
To a family that was burdened already
With enough of it.
I wish to go back to that house
Which saved the little girl
The pain of being unwanted.

I wish to go back and relive
Each of those moments when
I was a little girl,
For I was special and beautiful and important
In all of them.
I was the child which I never got to be again.
Now, I wish, I could go back in time,
For the time, when I had everything,
Because little did I know back then,
I would loose it all to time.

SOMETHING

In the lowest times and loneliest nights,
When my heart craves comfort,
There's something in me
Which always takes me back
To my good music collection;
A sincere list of selected songs
Which can pull me out
Of the deepest swamps of self hate.
Music has always been and will always be
My teacher; my guide; my mirror; my soul.

BEING ON PINS AND NEEDLES

Anticipation builds hype only to reveal disappointment. It's like the disappointment that you get after you tear open an attractive gift wrap that beautifully hides the dullness of a thoughtless last moment present. It's like the disrespect that you feel when someone's brilliantly chosen big words fail to deliver the compensation for their little understanding of you and your real personality. It's like the indifferent feeling that you get when you reach the much awaited destination after having endured a very difficult journey and it comes to your realization that maybe like you, everyone once believed that they were going to make a difference, but every possible opportunity and every possible direction ultimately brings everyone to the same place; from being someone to being like everyone, and finally a no-one.

LAST RESORT

This argument feels like a waste
Of the limited time
Which we have
Together.
Let's not try to seek conclusion this time
Because I know,
It will end
With only one of us winning.
Let me continue with my lie,
I'll let you live with your truth,
And together we can coexist
Peacefully in oblivion.

ABSENCE

Sometimes in a journey together,
Somewhere we realize that, "together"
Isn't, maybe the best situation to be in.
Instead of slowing down
In each other's presence,
We try to reach the finish line
In each other's absence.
Then at some point during the journey,
When we're far too alone,
When it's late to act,
We come to understand
That life played us all the same.

FOE

I was given a second chance
And I blew it too.
Well, I thought,
"I'm not good enough for you".
I felt judged and scared,
I still wanted to share,
But you didn't watch your tone.
And I went through the trauma
Alone.

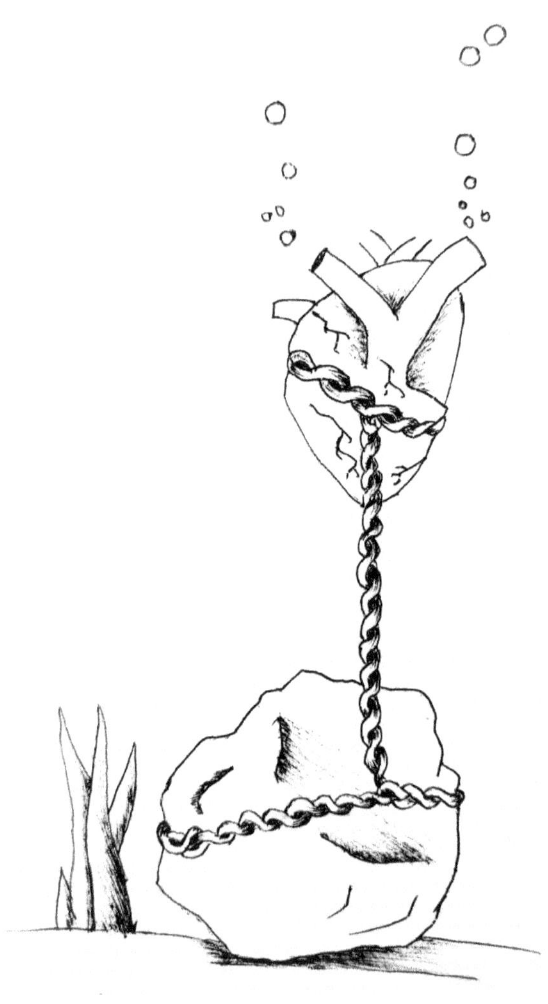

ROCK BOTTOM

I decided to swallow the words
Which would've burned down their ego,
And with it, our future, present and past.
I kept quiet.
So quiet that my lips forgot to move
And I never smiled.
I decided to bury all the replies within me,
But all it gave me was a heavy heart.
So heavy that I drowned and hit rock bottom.
And I decided to soak in the negativity.
I got so full of it,
That I didn't even struggle to catch my breath
Because I'd already started to decay before my time.

JUST A SECOND FIDDLE

My satisfaction and my sereneness
Must have been a baffling riddle
To those who tried to ridicule me
By calling me "Just a second fiddle".
My patience, my gratitude,
My selfless attitude,
My genuine smile,
My moderate stride,
All misunderstood for being too soft.
But I was just happy to be who I was.
Someone's kin, someone's friend,
Someone's backup, someone's sidekick,
I was just happy to be a helping hand.

REST

I want to be completely dry,
Ðrained of every emotion.
I want to cut loose the threads
Of the lies keeping me
Entangled in its mesh.
I want to free myself from
The burden of expectations
Crushing my chest.
Feels like forever
Because I've been uncomfortably stressed,
Now, I only want to rest.

LABELS

Pleasing, convincing or not?
Why do you compare?
If you want to believe it's day, it is day.
What anyone else says,
Why do you care?
You must discard all labels.
You must select an ink of your choosing.
If you want it to be pink,
Well, why not!
Stop overthinking,
Grab that pen,
Inscribe your name in your handwriting,
For it is your diary and your name,
And tell me then,
Pleasing, convincing or not?

TAKING CONTROL

Their kindness is a new feeling,
But little by little
What I've been stealing
Is the control which I had
Given away with my surrender.
They reminded me of my helplessness
Like a stubborn itch.
My body objected to their heinousness
With a sudden twitch.
And now, they've decided to be kind.
So, just like them,
I have also left the past behind.
With control up my sleeve
And experiences in my mind,
I have sensibly chosen
To leave my past behind.

ONE DAY

I saw but didn't say
I stayed then went astray
I knew they thought
That I was done
And they thought they'll always
Have their way
But hey! I'm here,
To take their pride away
Because I vowed that
I'll be back one day.

TEARS AND SMILES

Smile is a door
Which I shut on their faces,
And they never learn
The truth about me.
Tears are my secrets
Which I show
To the one who is persistent
And knocks to see,
If I am really okay.

FRIEND

I've had my share of loneliness,
And my heart kept searching love,
All I ever sang
Were the sad verses,
From my journal,
Where I had them shoved.
And, then I met you,
You were really kind to me,
You hushed my sobs and calmed me down,
I stopped being a misery.
I wish, we could all be kind to one another,
For life might never be kind enough,
And while we try to better each other,
Maybe, a little life will happen to us.

WHENEVER YOU COMPLETE MY SENTENCES

"Exactly", is what I usually say,
Whenever you complete my sentences.
I've known you longer than a decade,
Yet it feels just like yesterday.
While crying, laughing and sharing together,
We found comfort in one another.
It feels unreal to have found a soul
Who resonates with me,
Who makes me whole.
Now there are fewer surprises,
But when I give it a thought
More often than not,
My heart skips a beat
Whenever you complete my sentences.

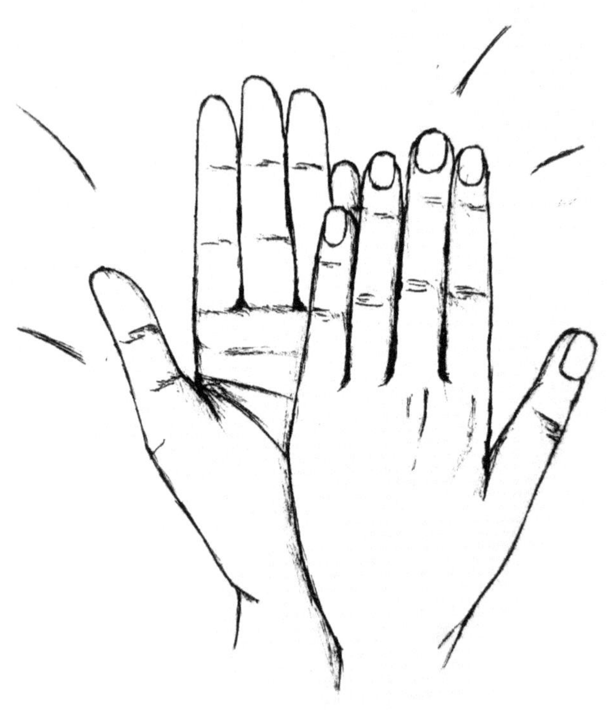

THE TWO OF US TOGETHER

I know the weather isn't that pretty
And the ride isn't going smoothly too,
Everyday doesn't need sunshine
Sometimes the rains will do.
There are gloomy days and lonely nights,
And it seems, it's the end of the line,
But, as long as we are together,
I know everything will be just fine.
Who cares if it's not going perfectly,
Who wants it all to be true,
I know that I've made it through,
And no matter what, I've got you.
It has been like a dream
Ever since we met.
The two of us together
Are singing an endless duet.

A STREAM

As colorless as it could be
It still has a hint of the sky.
As carefree as a nomad
It just passes by.
As narrow as it has to be,
It's got all the length to stretch,
As shallow as it may seem,
It still has the depth
That's good enough to submerge,
And satisfy my urge,
And sully the name of the scorching sun.

FREE AND TRAPPED

Clinking glasses of pina colada
Like high-fiving back in the days,
Gossips and giggles all mixed up
Like drinks mixed in a summer cocktail.
I realised the passing of life through me
As I tried to get hold of the sand,
Slowly slipping through my hand.
A smile gently danced on my lips,
Similar to the sunlit waves bouncing
Liberally to flaunt their curves and tips.
There's a continuous countdown;
At this moment, I feel immense freedom
To think, to feel, to let myself drown,
And as I am caught deep inside this feeling,
I realize, this moment is escaping me
Just like time itself.
Well, I know it's going to end sometime,
But for this while, when I am
Still seeking fidelity,
I feel free and I feel trapped.

STORIES

A STORYTELLER

The confusion in a painter's mind;
Failing to choose which colors to fill,
The thoughts of a potter at the time
When the moment calls to hold still,
The urgency in a beloved's confession
Minutes before parting away,
The tenacity of a husband's request
In attempt to get his wife to stay.
About a salesman's gimmick
Or about the problems of a brat,
About a magician's trick
Or maybe, about a lover's spat.
Go on and tell me
What you wish to hear today
And I will tell you another good story.

DEAR BEST FRIEND

Even though I don't believe in destiny,
I feel fortunate everyday
That you chose me.
And, even though I met
With absence mostly,
In the abundance of your company,
I heel a little everyday,
One wound at a time.

DEAR SISTER

Your relationship with your mother
Over the years has gotten better.
After all those cold wars and complains,
You understand her compulsion and pain
And there's no confusion of right and wrong,
You, my sister, have grown up well and strong.

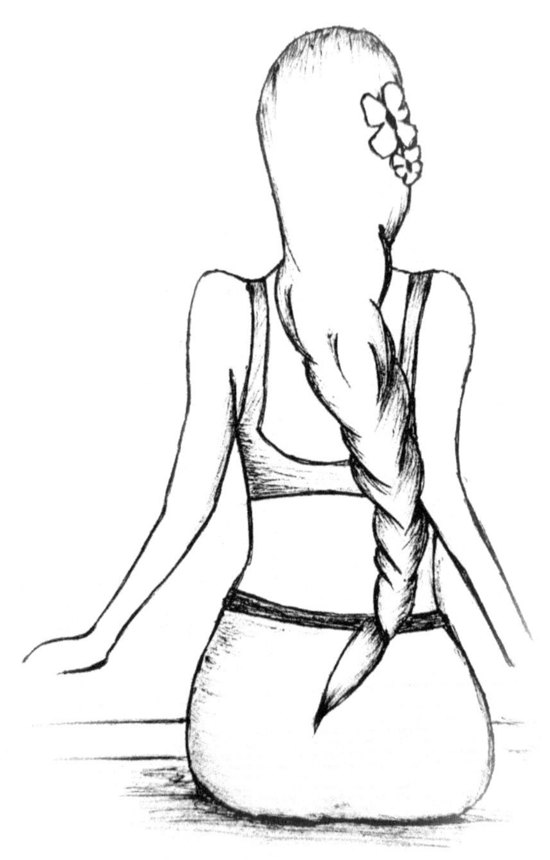

My Women

I'm the voice of the women
Who listened without complaints.
I'm the choice of the women
Who followed all restraints.
I'm the freedom of the women
Who desired it from a distance.
I'm the revenge of the women
Who always questioned their existence.
I'm the daughter of the woman
Who didn't hold me back like she was held.
I'm the sister of the women
Who didn't judge me when they were compelled.
I'm the friend of the women
Who've promised me trust and honesty.
I live through them and they live through me.

Individuality

We despise imperfections,
We suppress curiosity,
We chase perfection
And suffocate audacity.
Why?
Just so that we can be
Like everyone else.

SOLIDARITY

Possession, position, prestige, prize,
Every bite of the pie,
Only for ourselves.
How much is too much?
What is the extent of self-love?
At what point does it become selfishness?
The joy of sharing,
The intimacy in caring,
The rhythm of our steps together in marching,
The closeness, safety and all the other things
That came into being;
Only together.
You know how much they matter.
All things said,
I've come to believe that
Choosing solitude is good any day,
But living with solidarity is a much better way.

Taking it One Day at a Time

Life is much like the process of your clean face suddenly growing a cystic acne, turning it into a pigmented spot and then slowly clearing it up but never letting it disappear completely. Meanwhile, you get better at hiding it under make-up. This cycle leaves you with multiple faded spots and a low self esteem. A clean face seems like a childhood dream, but you eventually grow up, you learn that maturity and peace of mind is in accepting your face with the spots and yourself with all the positives and negatives of your personality, while simultaneously trying to work at the source of the problem. It is only with time that you understand that the problem is not with the spots, for acne is your body's way of communicating with you. The problem is your unfortunate circumstances and bad lifestyle choices.

Life is a process. At no point in life, can you be certain of who you really are and what defines you. You are ever changing and always evolving.

TIME COINS

When time is really all we have
To spend,
Then let's spend it wisely
On the things we enjoy doing together.
And, while breathing is still free,
Let's fill our lungs each time
With as much air as we possibly can
And make every breath count.

PASSING THROUGH

To the forests in search of wilderness,
To the valleys in search of peace,
To explore my creativity for hours,
To someday, discover my niche.
To delve into good books,
So that my mind gets to ponder.
To stroll through the city,
So that my heart gets to wander.
Passing through the highs and lows,
I will seek endlessly,
With content and excitement within,
What more life has for me.

Conformism

I will not run your race.
Wherever I go, I see people clustered in groups.
The need to fit in
Has divided us into these groups of people.
Groups have a common friend,
Groups have a common enemy,
Groups have a common agenda,
Groups have a common propaganda.
I see myself as free.
Free to choose that
I will not run your race.

I'M MY OWN PERSON

I'm all in for laughs,
I'm all in for tears,
I wish to be listened,
For you I'm all ears,
I'm open arms,
I'm closed gate,
I don't hesitate to love,
I don't mind your hate.

ON THE SAME WAVELENGTH

He said to her the other night,
How extremely lucky was he,
To know her ' coz she tries to understand
And does not pretend to agree.
She does not rush to form a judgement
And listens carefully,
She is not afraid to contradict him,
And always chooses her words wisely.
He said he feels really lucky
To have found someone like her,
He asked her to always be with him,
To always be together.
She said to him that she senses mutual respect
When she is in his company,
And her attitude is the reflected glory
Of his charm and his generosity.
She vowed to be with him through thick and thin
And assured him that she'll always be with him.
They promised friendship, respect and love to each
other,
They promised to be on the same wavelength,
They promised to always be together.

PURPOSE

In search of sympathy,
I found self love.
And in the quest for liberty
I found something
That is placed far above.
Purpose; a light at the end of a dark tunnel
Which will guide not just me
But will also help others to see
The possibility after misfortune,
And to dream
When everything seems out of tune.

ALL TOGETHER

Oh, how many nights I've spent awake!
Nothing but thinking,
Giggles and sobs,
Nostalgia and foresight,
Everything,
All together,
Bittersweet!

Dear Reader,

 With all the gratitude in my heart, I thank you for choosing my book! I hope you found something valuable in it; could be comfort, assurance or simply a relatable friend. If you liked or didn't like my poetry or just want to connect, you could visit my Instagram profile: @mansizmusingz or E-mail me at: mansichauhan240795@gmail.com. Your feedback and suggestions would motivate me to write more passionately.

Thank you again!

www.ingramcontent.com/pod-product-compliance
Lightning Source LLC
Chambersburg PA
CBHW041338120726
48005CB00014B/2303